AUDIO ACCESS
INCLUDED

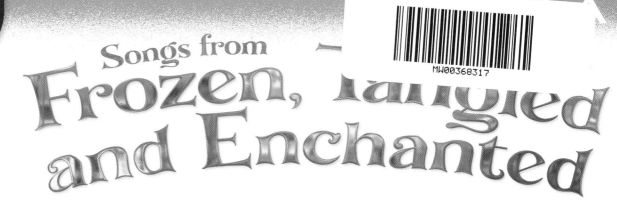

Songs from
Frozen, Tangled
and Enchanted

CONTENTS

To access audio visit:
www.halleonard.com/mylibrary

Enter Code
3376-9497-4533-2659

Audio Arrangements by Peter Deneff

ISBN 978-1-4803-8729-4

Disney characters and artwork © Disney Enterprises, Inc.

WALT DISNEY MUSIC COMPANY
WONDERLAND MUSIC COMPANY, INC.

DISTRIBUTED BY

7777 W. BLUEMOUND RD. P.O. BOX 13819 MILWAUKEE, WI 53213

In Australia Contact:
Hal Leonard Australia Pty. Ltd.
4 Lentara Court
Cheltenham, Victoria, 3192 Australia
Email: ausadmin@halleonard.com.au

Visit Hal Leonard Online at
www.halleonard.com

DO YOU WANT TO BUILD A SNOWMAN?

from Disney's Animated Feature FROZEN

VIOLA

Music and Lyrics by KRISTEN ANDERSON-LOPEZ
and ROBERT LOPEZ

FOR THE FIRST TIME IN FOREVER

from Disney's Animated Feature FROZEN

VIOLA

Music and Lyrics by KRISTEN ANDERSON-LOPEZ
and ROBERT LOPEZ

HAPPY WORKING SONG

from Walt Disneys Pictures' ENCHANTED

Music by ALAN MENKEN
Lyrics by STEPHEN SCHWARTZ

VIOLA

8

I SEE THE LIGHT
from Walt Disney Pictures' TANGLED

VIOLA

Music by ALAN MENKEN
Lyrics by GLENN SLATER

9

poco rit.   a tempo

rit.   *mp*

I'VE GOT A DREAM
from Walt Disney Pictures' TANGLED

VIOLA

Music by ALAN MENKEN
Lyrics by GLENN SLATER

11

IN SUMMER
from Disney's Animated Feature FROZEN

VIOLA

Music and Lyrics by KRISTEN ANDERSON-LOPEZ
and ROBERT LOPEZ

Easy 2 feel swing

LET IT GO
from Disney's Animated Feature FROZEN

VIOLA

Music and Lyrics by KRISTEN ANDERSON-LOPEZ
and ROBERT LOPEZ

15

LOVE IS AN OPEN DOOR

from Disney's Animated Feature FROZEN

VIOLA

Music and Lyrics by KRISTEN ANDERSON-LOPEZ
and ROBERT LOPEZ

MOTHER KNOWS BEST

from Walt Disney Pictures' TANGLED

VIOLA

Music by ALAN MENKEN
Lyrics by GLENN SLATER

SO CLOSE
from Walt Disney Pictures' ENCHANTED

VIOLA

Music by ALAN MENKEN
Lyrics by STEPHEN SCHWARTZ

Moderately, with feeling

THAT'S HOW YOU KNOW

from Walt Disney Pictures' ENCHANTED

Music by ALAN MENKEN
Lyrics by STEPHEN SCHWARTZ

VIOLA

TRUE LOVE'S KISS

from Walt Disney Pictures' ENCHANTED

VIOLA

Music by ALAN MENK
Lyrics by STEPHEN SCHWA

WHEN WILL MY LIFE BEGIN

from Walt Disney Pictures' TANGLED

VIOLA

Music by ALAN MENKEN
Lyrics by GLENN SLATER